I0792874

SERMON OUTLINES

on

New Testament Bible Characters

Also by Al Bryant

Climbing the Heights
Day by Day with C. H. Spurgeon
New Every Morning
Sermon Outlines on the Attributes of God
Sermon Outlines on Christ's Death, Resurrection, and Return
Sermon Outlines on the Cross of Christ
Sermon Outlines on the Deeper Life
Sermon Outlines for Evangelistic Services
Sermon Outlines on Faith, Hope, and Love
Sermon Outlines on the Family and Home
Sermon Outlines on the Fruit of the Spirit
Sermon Outlines for Funerals and Other Special Services
Sermon Outlines on the Grace of God
Sermon Outlines on the Holy Spirit
Sermon Outlines for Lay Leaders
Sermon Outlines on the Life of Christ
Sermon Outlines on New Testament Bible Characters
Sermon Outlines on Old Testament Bible Characters
Sermon Outlines on Paul's Letter to the Romans
Sermon Outlines on Prayer and Spiritual Living, vols. 1 & 2
Sermon Outlines on Prophetic Themes
Sermon Outlines on the Psalms
Sermon Outlines on Revival Themes
Sermon Outlines for Special Occasions, vols. 1 & 2
Sermon Outlines for Worship Services

SERMON OUTLINES

on

New Testament Bible Characters

compiled by

Al Bryant

Kregel Publications

Grand Rapids, MI 49501

Sermon Outlines on New Testament Bible Characters by Al Bryant

Copyright © 1992 by Kregel Publications, a division of Kregel, Inc., 2450 Oak Industrial Dr. NE, Grand Rapids, MI 49505.

All rights reserved. No part of this book may be reproduced, stored in a retrieval system, or transmitted in any form or by any means—electronic, mechanical, photocopy, recording, or otherwise—without written permission of the publisher, except for brief quotations in printed reviews.

Library of Congress Cataloging-in-Publication Data
Bryant, Al (1926–
Sermon outlines on New Testament Bible characters / [compiled by] Al Bryant.
p. cm.
Includes index.
1. Bible. N.T.—Biography—Sermons—Outlines, syllabi, etc. I. Bryant, Al, 1926–
BS2431.S475 1992 251'.01—dc20 91-21655
CIP

ISBN 978-0-8254-2095-5

4 5 6 7 8 / 19 18 17 16 15

Printed in the United States of America

CONTENTS

PREFACE

That highly regarded "preacher's preacher," Dr. Warren W. Wiersbe, has this to say about biographical preaching: "It is . . . perhaps the most rewarding, and yet the most difficult, kind of pulpit ministry. The Bible is a *Who's Who* of people who met God, knew God, trusted God, and either glorified Him or grieved Him. People identify with people. The men and women found in the Bible are just like the men and women in our homes and churches today. Anybody can meet himself or herself in the Bible." He goes on to point out, "That's what biographical preaching is all about—turning old portraits into modern 'moving pictures' and making dead people live and great truths come alive to help us serve God better today."

The sermon outlines in this book have been selected to help you make "dead people live" and "great truths come alive." The compiler has gone back to the works of such pulpit greats as Jabez Burns and F. E. Marsh to find their most provocative messages on New Testament characters from the old prophetess, Anna, and blind Bartimaeus all the way to the parables of the Rich Farmer and the Unprofitable Servant.

Also included is a series of sermons on the people of the parables Jesus told, another series on the person and ministry of Jesus Christ, and various facets of the life of Paul.

As in the other books of this series of ready-to-use sermon outlines, it is the compiler's prayer that you will find these messages relevant and timely in your own ministry.

While the outlines are quite complete and thorough, it is our hope that you will add the results of your own personal study into these fascinating lives to make these people peculiarly your own. It is also possible that a particular outline will lend itself to more than one message as you embellish these outlines with your own research and further study.

The New Testament is a gallery of interesting and enlightening people, in addition to being a solid doctrinal foundation for our faith. May the outlines in this collection enrich and enliven your own preaching ministry, as well as inform and challenge your people.

Al Bryant

TEXTUAL INDEX

ANNA

"Sometimes the sun seems to hang for half an hour in the horizon, only just to show how glorious it can be. The day is gone, the fervor of the shining is over, and the sun hangs golden—nay, redder than gold—in the west, making everything look unspeakably beautiful with the rich luster which it sheds on every side. So God seems to let some people, when their duty in this world is done, hang in the west, that men may look on them, and see how beautiful they are." Such a person was the aged Anna.

1. **Anna was a prophetess (Luke 2:36).**

As a prophet was one who received messages from God, through being in immediate communication with Him, so a prophetess was the same. Dr. Bullinger says, "The usage of the word is clear, it signifies one on whom the Spirit of God rested (Num. 11:17, 25,26, 29); one to whom and through whom God speaks (Num. 12:2); one to whom God makes known His mysteries (Amos 3:7,8). Hence it means one to whom God reveals His truth, and through whom He speaks" (Gen. 20:7, 17,18).

2. **Anna was a servant of God (Luke 2:37).**

It is said of her that she "served God." What better epitaph could one have, than a testimony of having served the Lord? "Ye serve the Lord Christ" (Col. 3:24) was the apostle's word to the Christian slaves at Colosse as he urged them to do their menial tasks as unto the Lord Himself.

A carpenter was once asked why he troubled to finish off a magistrate's bench so carefully. His reply was, "I can't do otherwise; besides, I may have to sit on it one of these days." A better reply was given by the little servant girl when she was asked why she took such pains in washing the kitchen floor, "I am doing it for the Lord Jesus." Ah! if anything be done for, and as to, Him it will be done well.

3. **Anna was self-denying.**

It is said she fasted (Luke 2:37). Anna did not fast, as some do, to obtain favor with God, but, knowing the grace of the Lord, she was willing to deny herself food that she might serve the Lord better.

4. **Anna was prayerful (Luke 2:37).**

Her prayers ascended to God "night and day." She was incessant in her pleading, and attentive in her attendance at the means of grace. An old writer says, "Prayer is the *key* of the morning and the *lock* of the evening." If we pray each morning before we go out on life's pathway, we shall unlock the mercies God has for us; and if we look to Him at the close of the day, we shall know that we are locked in with God from all harm and evil, as Noah was when the Lord shut him in the ark.

5. Anna was thankful.

Simeon was not alone in his thanksgiving, for Anna "gave thanks likewise unto the Lord" (Luke 2:38). Praise is comely to the Lord. Those who bless God with their praises are sure to be blessed by God with His mercies. A thankful man is full of blessing. To be thankless is to be graceless, but to be thankful is to be graceful.

6. Anna was a true witness.

"She spake of Him" (Luke 2:38). Her testimony of Christ as the Redeemer is implied in that she "spake of Him to all that looked for *redemption* in Jerusalem." A true witness always testifies as to who Christ is, what He has done, and what He is able to do, as known from personal experience.

F. E. MARSH

CORNELIUS

1. A *religious* man	"A devout man . . ."	Acts 10:2
2. A *reverent* man	"One that feared God."	v. 2
3. A *praying* man	"Prayed to God always."	v. 2
4. An *influential* man	"Of good report . . . nation."	v. 22
5. A *liberal* man	"Gave much alms."	v. 2
6. An *enquiring* man	"What is it, Lord?"	v. 4
7. A *privileged* man	"Saw in a vision."	v. 3
8. A *teachable* man	"Here . . . of God."	v. 33
9. A *saved* man	"Whereby thou . . . saved."	Acts 11:14

INGLIS

BLIND BARTIMAEUS

Luke 18:35-43

Observe,

I. The Circumstances and Situation of Bartimaeus

A. *He was blind.* Deprived of the invaluable sense of seeing; stranger to the beauties of nature; incapable of enjoying the pleasant light of the sun; deprived of all the pleasures and profits of reading; in a state of imminent peril.

B. *He was poor.* Not able to pursue any worldly calling; dependent on the alms of the passing traveler.

C. *His case was, humanly speaking, hopeless.* Let these observations be applied to the natural state of men in their unregenerate condition. Understanding darkened, spiritually poor, and beyond the power of human energy to restore (Eph. 2:1,2; 11:12).

Notice,

II. His Application to Christ

A. *Two indispensable occurrences preceded this:*

1. Christ passed that way. The blind man's condition rendered it impossible that he should have sought the Savior.
2. He was informed that it was Jesus who now approached, or still the Friend of sinners might have passed on, without the knowledge of that circumstance. So, in like manner, Christ has passed by us; He has come near to us—become our dear kinsman—sought us out; or we never could have received His salvation.

B. *Having noticed these preliminary circumstances, we observe that his application to Christ was—*

1. *An application for mercy.* Not demanded as his right, but sought as mercy. He felt his misery, knew his unworthiness, and therefore, sought mercy. It was—
2. *The application of faith.* He addressed Christ as the Savior, "Jesus." He honored Him as the expected Messiah, "Son of David." While rulers and priests proclaimed Him as an impostor and Pharisees denounced Him as a sinner, and attributed His

miracles to Satanic agency, this poor man addressed Him as Israel's long-expected deliverer, the Savior of the world, and believed He possessed power to restore his sight: "Jesus, thou Son of David, have mercy on me." It was,

3. *Ardent and persevering application*. He continued to cry; and he ceased not until his cry was heard, and his petition granted.

Observe,

III. The Result of This Application

A. The people tried to silence him. Bartimaeus cried out the more earnestly. Let seeking sinners imitate him.

1. *Jesus stood still*. Prayer stopped Him in His course; the blind man's cry of misery fastened Him to the spot.
2. *He commanded him to be brought*. Prayer brings the soul near to Christ.
3. *He inquired his request*. Not that He was ignorant, but to give Bartimaeus an opportunity of presenting his plea.
4. *He granted his soul's desire*. "Receive thy sight."
5. *He honored his faith*. "Thy faith hath saved thee." Not by any inherent power or meritorious influence, but by bringing his illness to the right physician, by laying hold of the only Savior. He had honored Christ by his faith, and now Christ honors that faith before the people. Ephesians 2:8.

Observe,

IV. The Course Bartimaeus Adopted

A. *He followed Christ*. As a monument of His mercy; witness of and for His truth; as grateful for the blessing conferred. Christ expects all His disciples to follow Him. To let their light shine, etc.

B. *He glorified God*. By acknowledgment, praise, and dedication. And finally, "the people also gave praise to God."

JABEZ BURNS

CHRIST BEFORE THE BELIEVER

1. As the *Object* of faith. "Looking unto Jesus the Author and Finisher of our faith" (Heb. 12:2).
2. As the *Light*, to direct. "He that followeth Me shall not walk in darkness" (John 8:12).
3. As the *Lord*, to obey. "If I then, your Lord and Master, have washed your feet; ye also ought to wash one another's feet" (John 13:14).
4. As the *Shepherd*, to follow. "My sheep hear My voice and I know them and they follow Me" (John 10:27).
5. As the *Master*, to serve. "Ye call Me Master and Lord: and ye say well; for so I am" (John 13:13).
6. As the *Prize*, to win. "For whom I have suffered the loss of all things, . . . that I may win Christ" (Phil. 3:8-14).
7. As the *Goal*, to reach. "Know ye not that they which run in a race run all, but one receiveth the prize? So run, that ye may obtain" (1 Cor. 9:24). F. E. MARSH

CHRIST BEHIND THE BELIEVER

1. As the *Suffering One* for us. "Once . . . He appeared to put away sin" (Heb. 9:26).
2. As the *Pillar of fire*, for light and protection. "It was a cloud and darkness to them, but it gave light by night to these" (Ex. 14:20).
3. As the *Voice, to direct*. "Thine ears shall hear a word behind thee, saying, this is the way" (Isa. 30:21).
4. As the *Beloved, to encourage*. "He looketh forth at the windows, shewing Himself" (Song 2:9).
5. As the *Goodness and mercy, to follow*. "Surely goodness and mercy shall follow me all the days of my life" (Ps. 23:6).
6. As the *Lord, to reveal*. "I heard a voice behind me" (Rev. 1:10).
7. As our *Reward, for separation* between us and the world. "The God of Israel will be your Reward" (Isa. 52:12).

F. E. MARSH

CHRIST BENEATH THE BELIEVER

1. As the *Foundation* on whom we are built. "For other Foundation can no man lay" (1 Cor. 2:11).
2. As the *Way* to walk in. "I am the Way" (John 14:6).
3. As the *Shoes* of Peace, to protect. "Your feet shod with the preparation of the Gospel of peace" (Eph. 6:15).
4. As the *Arms* to carry. "Underneath are the everlasting arms" (Deut. 33:27).
5. As the *Shoulders* to bear. "Layeth it on His shoulders" (Luke 15:5).
6. As the *Bosom* to rest in. "Which also leaned on His breast" (John 21:20).
7. As the *Staff* to support. "Thy rod and Thy staff" (Ps. 23:4).

F. E. MARSH

CHRIST BESIDE THE BELIEVER

1. As the *Strength* to uphold. "I will uphold thee with the right hand of My righteousness" (Isa. 41:10).
2. As the *Companion*, for fellowship. "Did not our heart burn within us, while He talked with us by the way" (Luke 24:32).
3. As the *Friend* to counsel. "The sweetness of man's friend by hearty counsel" (Prov. 27:9).
4. As the *Guide*, to direct. "When He, the Spirit of Truth, is come, He will guide you into all truth" (John 16:13).
5. As the *High Priest*, to succor. "We have not an High Priest which cannot be touched with the feeling of our infirmities" (Heb. 4:15).
6. As the *Comforter*, to cheer. "He shall give you another Comforter, that He may abide with you forever" (John 14:16).
7. As the *Teacher*, to teach. "He shall teach you all things, and bring all things to your remembrance" (John 14:26).

F. E. MARSH

CHRIST FOR US

Different characters in which Christ appears for us in Hebrews 9 and 10.

1. As the *Propitiation*, to atone (Heb. 9:12).
2. As the *Purifier*, to cleanse (9:14).
3. As the *Mediator*, to act (9:15).
4. As the *Priest*, to represent (9:24).
5. As the *Sin-Remover*, to bless (9:26).
6. As the *Substitute*, to suffer (9:28).
7. As the *Savior*, to deliver (9:28).
8. As the *Willing One* in obedience (10:5-9).
9. As the *Sanctifier*, to separate (10:10).
10. As the *Sin-offering*, to save (10:11,12).
11. As the *Exalted Man* in glory (10:12).
12. As the *Expectant One*, to triumph (10:13).
13. As the *Perfecter* of His people (10:14).
14. As the *Forerunner*, to procure (10:19,20).
15. As the *High Priest*, to represent (10:21).

F. E. MARSH

CHRIST'S GLORY

John 2:11

As the first ray of the morning sun is the harbinger of the sunshine of the day, so this first miracle was the forerunner of the many wondrous deeds that Christ was about to perform.

There are many rays in the sun of Christ's glory:

1. The *moral* glory of His *life* proclaims the *spotlessness* of His *holiness* (John 1:14).
2. The *majestic* glory of His *person* speaks forth the *excellence* of His *worth* (2 Peter 1:17).
3. The *mysterious* glory of His Deity *tells* out the *wonder* of His *Godhead* (Ps. 24:7, 10; Heb. 1:3).
4. The *munificent* glory of His *grace* reminds us of the *greatness* of His *mercy* (Eph. 1:6).
5. The *many-sided* glory of His *truth* declares the *immutability* of its *infallibility* (Ps. 108:4,5).
6. The *marvelous* glory of His *Gospel* tells out the *sufficiency* of His *atonement* (2 Cor. 4:6).
7. The *mighty* glory of His *miracles* speaks of the *strength* of His *power* (Eph. 3:16, 19).

F. E. MARSH

GOOD OLD SIMEON

"And, behold, there was a man in Jerusalem, whose name was Simeon; and the same man was just and devout, waiting for the consolation of Israel; and the Holy Ghost was upon him. And it was revealed unto him by the Holy Ghost, that he should not see death, before he had seen the Lord's Christ" (Luke 2:25-30).

There are two or three scenes most beautiful and interesting in nature—

The setting sun, going down in a clear sky, in all its magnificence and glory. It is lit up with its declining beams, and setting grandeur.

The field ripe for the harvest. The golden waving corn, with its teeming abundance, inviting the active hand of the reaper.

The ship in full sail, within sight of her destined port. The sea crossed, the toils and perils of the voyage over, and friends on shore, ready to welcome the crew and passengers to their native shores.

In the death of the aged Christian, all these interesting features are beautifully exhibited. As a moral sun: he now sets on earth, to arise and shine in the sphere of glory. As a shock of corn: he is ripe and ready for the garner of eternal life. As a gallant vessel: he has neared the shores of immortality, and an abundant entrance is about to be ministered into the haven of celestial blessedness.

Such was the character and circumstances of good old Simeon, as exhibited in the text. Let us consider,

I. *His Religious Character*.

Here observe,

A. *His evangelical faith*.

"Waiting for the consolation of Israel," that is, for the Messiah—the Savior. He believed in the Prophecies—Promises—Types, etc., relating to the Messiah. It excited his desires and hopes, and influenced his character. "He waited."

B. *He was righteous in life*.

"Just." A man of integrity and uprightness. No religion without this. "Do ye unto others," etc. Thus before God and with men he was unblamable.

C. *He had a devout spirit*.

A man of religious emotion—of worship and prayer.

These three are ever essential to true saving piety. Here is right principle—upright conduct—and spiritual emotion.

Observe,

II. ***His Distinguished Privileges.***

A. *His supernatural gift.*

"The Holy Ghost was upon him." As formerly on the prophets. It had ceased for nearly 400 years, but was now specially imparted to Simeon.

B. *His express revelation.*

It was revealed that before he saw death, he should see the Savior—Jehovah's Christ; the anointed—the Lord.

C. *His delightful interview.*

The period had now arrived. Simeon was led by the Spirit into the temple, etc. Then the holy child, Jesus, was brought in. Oh, think of the place, and the meeting! and how God brought it about!

D. *His reception of Jesus.*

"Saw Him." "Took Him in his arms," etc. Thus faith and love receive Christ. It is not Christ in the manger, or on the cross, or in heaven; but in the arms of faith and love, that can save us, and make us happy. This leads us, then, to

III. ***His Holy Rapture.***

Observe the particulars of it:

A. *Gratitude to God.*

"Blessed God." Godly joy is ever grateful joy. His soul rose in holy exultation to the fountain of his privileges and blessings.

B. *His desired severance from the world.*

"Lord, now lettest," etc. All the ends of life he felt to be accomplished. World's attraction gone. Often persons wish to live for this and that end. The warrior—the statesman—the philosopher—the merchant—the parent. How imbecile, in general, these desires!

C. *His hallowed desires for glory.*

He longed now for the rest, and the bliss, of a better world. He had attained,

D. *The consummation of all his hopes.*

"For mine eyes have seen thy salvation," etc. Abraham saw Christ's day afar off. Jacob died waiting for it. David sang of it. Good old Simeon realized it.

JABEZ BURNS

THE GOOD SAMARITAN

There are many thoughts which are suggested if we take the Good Samaritan as a type of Christ (Luke 10:30-37).

I. **Condescension of the Good Samaritan.**

"He came where he was" (v. 33), unlike those who passed by on the other side. In like manner Christ came where we were.

He came to our *humanity*, and took it upon Him (Heb. 2:14). He came to our *sorrow*, and became acquainted with it (Isa. 53:4); He came to our *death*, and died it (1 Peter 3:18); He came to our *sin*, and bore it (2 Cor. 5:21); He came to our *curse*, and passed through it (Gal. 3:13); He came to our *woe*, and endured it (Heb. 12:2); and He came to our *lowness*, to lift us out of it (Phil. 2:8).

II. **Compassion of the Good Samaritan.**

"He had compassion on him" (v. 33). Repeatedly we read of Christ being moved with compassion in His life, but the kindness of His compassion was, when He took pity upon us, as He saw us in our sin (Ezek. 16:8), and died on our account (Rom. 5:6, 8), for as David had compassion on Mephibosheth, and brought him to his own house (2 Sam. 9), so Christ has had compassion upon us, in dying to meet our need.

III. **Care of the Good Samaritan.**

There are seven things the Good Samaritan did for the man.

A. He *"went to him."* He did not send a deputy to do his work. So with Christ. He *saves* (2 Tim. 1:9). He *gives* (John 14:27). He *sustains* (Isa. 41:10). He *accompanies* (Ex. 33:14), and He *keeps* (Jude 24).
B. He *"bound up his wounds."* So with Christ. He *heals* by His stripes (Isa. 53:5), and *comforts* by His grace (2 Cor. 12:9).
C. He *"poured in oil and wine."* So with Christ. He gives unction of His Spirit (1 John 2:27; 2 Cor. 1:21), and the wine of His joy (Ps. 104:15).
D. He *"set him on his own beast."* In like manner, Christ gives us to sit in the place where He had been (Eph. 2:6).
E. He *"brought him to an inn."* So Christ brings us to a

place of safety (Isa. 32:2), and into the banqueting house of His fellowship (Song of Sol. 2:4).

F. He *"took care of him."* So with Christ. Those who are taken up by Him are not given up. They are in His mighty grip (John 10:28), and cared for (1 Peter 5:7).

G. *He left supplies for the man.* "He took out two pence." What a supply we have in Christ (Eph. 1:3; Phil. 4:19).

F. E. MARSH

THE CRIPPLE AT THE BEAUTIFUL GATE

I. What the Man Was
   1. *Helpless*— "Laid daily at the gate."— Acts 3:2
   2. *Needy*— "To ask alms."— Acts 3:2
   3. *Expectant*— "Expecting . . . of them."— Acts 3:5

II. What the Man Realized
   1. *A marvelous change*— "Miracle of healing"— Acts 4:22
   2. *An instantaneous change*— "Immediately . . . strength."— Acts 2:7
   3. *A manifest*— "All . . . saw him."— Acts 2:9

III. What the Man Did
   1. *Walked*
   2. *Praised God*— "Walking and leaping and praising God."— Acts 2:8

INGLIS

JESUS AT THE GRAVE OF LAZARUS

I. **The Sympathy of Jesus (John 11:35).**

We might call this verse, "Jesus wept," the shortest verse in the Bible with the greatest meaning. The heart of Jesus ever beats in sympathy with the need of humanity, as His hand is ever ready to meet the need He sees. Spurgeon has well called this verse "a unique verse," and said, "I have often felt vexed with the man, whoever he was, who chopped up the New Testament into verses. He seems to have let the hatchet drop indiscriminately here and there, but I forgive him a great deal of blundering for his wisdom in letting these two words make a verse for themselves, 'Jesus wept.' This is a diamond of the first water, and it cannot have another gem set with it, for it is unique. Shortest of verses in words, but where is there a longer one in sense? Let it stand in solitary sublimity and simplicity."

Three times we read of Jesus weeping. He wept tears of personal suffering (Heb. 5:7), tears of compassion (Luke 19:41), and here tears of sympathy.

II. **The Command of Jesus (John 11:39).**

There was a work which those who were standing by the grave had to do, before Christ spoke the life-giving word that raised Lazarus from the dead, and that was to remove the stone which lay at the tomb's mouth. There are many stones that believers can roll away which keep the unsaved from hearing Christ's voice. Here are some stones to roll away:

The rocky stone of *ignorance*.
The granite stone of *unbelief*.
The slaty stone of *error*.
The lime-stone of *prejudice*.
The hard stone of *doubt*.
The slippery stone of *inconsistency*.
The dazzling stone of *fear*.

III. **The Power of Jesus (John 11:41-44).**

Disease, devils, and death had all to submit to Christ. The miracles of Christ in His earthly life are but illustrations of what He can do now in resurrection power by the Holy Spirit through the preaching of the Gospel. Those who are dead in ceremonialism

(Rev. 3:1) He can quicken; those who are buried in the pleasures of the world (1 Tim. 5:6) He can raise to delight in the pleasures that last for evermore (Ps. 16:11); those who are devoid of spiritual life and love, like the prodigal in the far country (Luke 15:24), He can robe and rejoice (Luke 15:22,23); and those who, like the Ephesians, are ruled by the powers of darkness (Eph. 2:1-3; Acts 19:19) He can raise to the heavenly places (Eph. 2:6), and make them fight against the powers that once held them in their grip (Eph. 6:12).

F. E. MARSH

BARNABAS IN THE ACTS

1.	He was *greatly* beloved	"Beloved Barnabas"	Acts 15:25
2.	He was *intensely* happy	"He was happy"	Acts 11:23
3.	He was a *gifted* exhorter	"He exhorted them"	Acts 11:23
4.	He was *filled* with power	"Full of the Holy Ghost"	Acts 11:24
5.	He was *strong* in faith	"Full of faith"	Acts 11:24
6.	He was very *fearless*	"Hazarded his life"	Acts 15:25-26
7.	He was always reliable	"Gifts entrusted to him"	Acts 15:35
8.	He was fully consecrated	"Laid all at the apostles' feet"	Acts 4:36-37

INGLIS

JESUS BEFORE THE HIGH PRIEST

Mark 14:53-64

If there is one thing more than another that impresses one in the life of Christ, it is the revealing power of His person, as He comes in contact with men. His presence was the searchlight to reveal men in their real characters.

Seven characteristics of Christ are seen in this portion of Scripture:

1. The Passive Victim.

"They led Jesus away" (v. 53; Isa. 53:7,8; Acts 8:32). There is no resistance on the part of Christ, but meekly and humbly He allows Himself to be led away. What majesty there is in His passiveness! With a look He could have made His enemies fall back (John 18:6); with a word He could have called twelve legions of angels to His aid (Matt. 26:53), and by His own power He could have escaped (Luke 4:30), but He wills to allow Himself to be in the hands of wicked men, that the purpose of God may be accomplished (Acts 2:23).

2. The Neglected Lord (v. 54).

Where now is Peter's willingness to go even to death with Christ (v. 29)? Instead of following close to the Lord (Ps. 63:8), Peter is following "afar off." Christ is neglected by the man who professed so much. How true are the insightful words of Cecil, "Our very virtues, left to themselves, bear us down, like weights to destruction."

3. The Falsely Accused (vv. 55-59).

There are three things about the false witnesses who spoke against Christ. They had to be sought or hired for the occasion; their witness was contradictory; and they told a lie in relation to the destruction of the Temple. If we compare John 2:19 with Mark 14:58, it will be found that Christ did not say that *He* would destroy the Temple, but if the *Jews* destroyed it, He would build it again in three days.

4. The Silent Savior (vv. 60,61).

"He opened not His mouth" to vindicate Himself. He might have defended Himself from His false accusers. How truly was "silence golden" in the case of Christ, and herein the Holy Spirit points Him out to us as our Example (see 1 Peter 2:21-23). Euripides was wont to say, "Silence was an answer to a wise man." What an answer we may see in the silence of Christ, if we are made wise by the Spirit of wisdom.

5. **The Blessed Christ (vv. 61,62).**

Christ never hesitated to answer when the question touched His Deity. For Him not to answer then, would be to betray Himself. There is no hesitation in the reply of Christ when the High Priest asks Him if He is "The Christ." Like a clear trumpet blast, the answer comes: "I Am." Thus Christ says He is The Great I AM (Ex. 3:14). It has often been said that Christians claim for Christ what He never claimed for Himself, namely, that He was God. But if the "I AM's" of Christ in the Gospel of John are studied, it will be seen that He claims to be God again and again.

6. **The Coming Man (v. 62).**

Christ proclaims that there is a day coming when He will be the Judge and not the judged; when Caiaphas will stand before Him, instead of Christ standing before Caiaphas; when the Prisoner will be the Potentate; when the Despised will be the Honored One; and when the Weak One shall come in power.

No truth is so prominent in the New Testament as the coming of the Lord Jesus, but of one thing we must be careful, and that is, to note the character in which He is coming. Here He says He will come as "The Son of Man," and hence in judgment (John 5:27), and not in grace, as when He comes as our Hope (1 John 3:2,3), and Savior (Phil. 3:20,21).

7. **The Condemned Man (v. 64).**

They condemned the Son of Man, and God the Son, as being guilty of blasphemy, and therefore, worthy of death. Can we not see beneath the hatred and cruelty of the authorities who condemned Christ to death, that He was delivered for our offenses (Rom. 4:25), that we might be freed from condemnation (Rom. 8:1), and be able to say, "Who is he that condemneth" (Rom. 8:34)?

F. E. MARSH

JESUS AND JOHN

We note a sevenfold contrast between John and Jesus.

1. John was the *messenger* of Christ.

Christ was the *One announced*. John went before to prepare for Christ's coming.

2. John was the *voice*.

Jesus was the *Word*. John was the voice that spoke the word. John Trapp says, "John was all voice. . . . his apparel, his diet, his conversation did preach holiness as well as his doctrine" (Mark 6:20). John was a true voice, for he spoke only of Jesus. He delighted to honor Him whom the Father honored. John is our example.

3. John was the *forerunner*.

Jesus was the *Lord*. John went before to announce the coming of Christ. His special mission was to reprove men of their sins, and to get them to repent of them (Matt. 3:6). Christ came to save men from their sins (Matt. 1:21).

4. John was the *herald*. Jesus was the *Person* spoken of.

On the Day of Jubilee the priests blew the silver trumpets, and as their clarion notes rang out they told the people of redemption for the slave, rest for the weary, release for the debtor, and rejoicing for the sad (Lev. 25); so John comes to herald the approach of Him who was to give infinitely more than the Year of Jubilee gave to the Israelites.

5. John was the *testifier*.

Jesus was the *Truth*. John's testimony was clear and pointed. He gave no uncertain sound. On one occasion he said, "Behold the Lamb of God, which taketh away the sin of the world" (John 1:29).

6. John was the *lamp*.

Christ was the *Light*. Christ says of Himself, "I am the Light of the World" (John 8:12), and of John He says, "He was a burning and shining *light*," or, as the Revised Version, "He was the *lamp* that burneth and shineth" (John 5:35). The word that Christ uses of Himself signifies light *underived*, as the light of the sun, hence that which shines by its own inherent power; but the word that Christ uses of John means the light of a lamp which is fed with oil, hence it is dependent upon something else for its being and shining. The lamp only burns as it is fed with oil. Could any two words describe in a more concise or clear manner the truth that Christ is the Light dependent upon none, and that the servant of Christ can only be a light as he receives from Christ? Christ is essentially the Light of all knowledge, the Light of all holiness, the Light of all grace, the Light of all Love, the Light of all power, the Light of all joy, the Light of all truth, the Light of all compassion, and the Light of all righteousness; but we are in ourselves the very opposite to all that Christ is, and we can only resemble Him in any small degree as He ministers to us the oil of the grace of the Holy Spirit. He is the Minister who attends to the needs of His saints that they may shine for Him, even as the priest in the tabernacle continually supplied the lamps of the lampstand with oil that they might never go out (Lev. 24:2,4).

7. John was the baptizer in *water*.

Jesus was and is the Baptizer in the *Holy Spirit* (John 1:33, R.V., M.).

F. E. MARSH

THE NAME OF JESUS IN HEBREWS

1. As *Son of Man*. "But we see *Jesus*, who was made a little lower than the angels for the suffering of death" (Heb. 2:9).
2. As our *High Priest*. "We have a great High Priest, who is passed into the heavens, *Jesus*, the Son of God" (Heb. 4:14, and 6:20).
3. As our *Surety* (or Security). "By so much was *Jesus* made a Surety of a better testament" (Heb. 7:22).
4. As the *Way into the holiest*. "Having, therefore, brethren, boldness to enter into the holiest by the blood of Jesus" (Heb. 10:19).
5. As the *Author of faith*. "Looking unto *Jesus*, the Author and Finisher of our faith" (Heb. 12:2).
6. As our *Mediator*. "And to *Jesus* the Mediator of the new covenant" (Heb. 12:24).
7. As our *Sanctifier*. "Wherefore *Jesus* also, that He might sanctify the people with His own blood, suffered without the gate" (Heb. 13:12).

F. E. MARSH

JOHN AND HEROD

Mark 6:14-29

Let us note a few contrasts between John and Herod.

I. John Was a Faithful Man; Herod Was a Faithless Man

The faithfulness of John is seen in that he rebuked Herod for living in sin (vv. 17,18). John was a man who had looked in the face of God; for that reason, he did not fear the frown of men. He who can speak with God in holy communion, will not fail in faithfulness to God, to tell men of their sins.

In contrast to John's faith*ful*ness we have Herod's faith*less*ness. In verse 20 we are told that Herod feared and observed John, heard him gladly, and did many things, but after all Herod was only a stony ground hearer (Mark 4:16,17). Spurgeon says of Herod, "Herod was a foxy man. We sometimes meet with these foxy people. They want to go to heaven, but they like the road to hell. They will sing a hymn to Jesus, but a good roaring song they like also. They will give money to the church, but how much money is spent on their own lust. They try and dodge between God and Satan. . . . Herod was like a bird taken with lime-twigs; he wanted to fly; but, sad to say, he was willingly held, limed by his lust."

II. John Was a Blessed Man; Herod Was a Burdened Man

John was blessed in many ways. *John was a blessed man because of his character*. He was *pure* in heart, like a cleansed vessel, free from all contamination. He was *holy* in life, like the tabernacle, he was set apart for God's indwelling and use; and he was *righteous* in action like an even balance, he did that which was right between men and God, and men and men. *John was a blessed man because he suffered for the sake of truth*. Those who suffer for the sake of Christ are blessed, as He Himself says (Matt. 5:11,12); their very shame is an occasion for rejoicing, as it is illustrated in the early Christians (Acts 5:41); and when any are called to seal their testimony with their death, they are blessed indeed, for they receive the martyr's crown of life (Rev. 2:10).

Herod was a burdened man. Herod was burdened in many ways. *He was burdened with his sins*. He was living a shameful life and he knew it, but for all that he would not quit his sins. A load of guilt was upon him, and his iniquities hung about him like a millstone.

Herod was burdened with a troubled conscience. When he heard of the miracles that Christ was doing, he thought that John had risen from the dead, and was troubled in consequence (vv. 14-17). When a man's sins haunt him, he has a host of ghosts which make him afraid, and well they may.

Joseph's brethren could not forget the sins they had committed against their brother. Twenty years later the memory of their action is still fresh (Gen. 42:21), yea, even later than that (Gen. 50:17). Shakespeare represents, in a striking manner, the accusation of a guilty conscience in his scene in "Macbeth," when he pictures Lady Macbeth trying to wash out the stain of blood from her hands.

There is one stone in the floor of an old church in Scotland which stares out at you blood-red from the gray stones around it. The legend tells of a murder committed there, and of repeated fruitless attempts to cover the tell-tale color of that stone. Morally the legend is true; every dead sin sends its ghosts to haunt the souls of the guilty. Committed sin is a *scar* that cannot be effaced, a *diamond-cut* that cannot be obliterated, a *mark* that cannot be rubbed out, a *stain* that cannot be washed out, an *impression* that is indelible, a *leak* that cannot be stopped, and a *burden* that cannot be removed—that is, from the human standpoint. All things are possible with God, through faith in the atonement of Christ. F. E. MARSH

THE LEPER IN MARK 1

I. A Sad Picture to be Studied.
   Leprosy resembles sin because:
   1. It separates
   2. It is loathsome
   3. It is deep-seated
   4. It is incurable by human power

II. A Glorious Example to be Imitated
   1. Imitate his *confession*— "Lord . . . clean"— v. 40
   2. Imitate his *attitude*— "Kneeling"— v. 40
   3. Imitate his *faith*— "Thou canst"— v. 40

III. A Striking Change to be Experienced
   1. It was *instantaneous*— "Immediately"— v. 42
   2. It was *manifest*— "He was cleansed"— v. 42

INGLIS

JOHN THE BAPTIST

Matthew 11:11

The life of John the Baptist was full of striking incident, and therefore, is well adapted, both to furnish instruction and edification to our minds. It will not be possible, however, in this profile, to do more than give a rapid view of the main features of his history and character. Observe, then,

I. *That He Was the Subject of Inspired Prediction.*

See Malachi 3:1. Here he is predicted under the title of "Jehovah's Messenger"—especially sent forth to prepare the way of the Lord, and act as a herald to the world's Messiah!

II. *His Birth Was Extraordinary and Supernatural.*

His parents were the godly Zacharias and Elizabeth. Both were aged, and his mother past the time of bearing children. Luke 1:5-7. God sent a special messenger to announce the designed event. Hence, as Zacharias ministered before the Lord, "an angel of the Lord appeared" (Luke 1:8-17). It will be seen, by reading the inspired narrative, that Zacharias was the cousin of our blessed Lord.

His name was given him, evidently, under supernatural direction. The name John signifies—"the gift," or "the grace," or "the mercy of the Lord"; and was very appropriate, as applied to John. Observe,

III. *The Spiritual Excellences of His Character.*

These we may fully learn from the prediction given of him by the angel—"He was to be filled with the Holy Ghost" (Luke 1:15). Sanctified by God from the womb. Hence he was eminently holy in his own person. A pure vessel for the Master's special use.

A. It was evident that he was to be particularly distinguished for seriousness of spirit. The fear of God was to be the predominant feature of his moral character.
B. He was characterized for great self-denial. His dress—his style of living—his abstinence from wine and luxuries; Luke 1:15.
C. He was also to be eminently humble. He was to be the servant. Not to affect pomp—not to glorify himself. Hence the striking evidence of his modesty, in hesitating to baptize the Redeemer; and confessing that he was

but the voice, sent to prepare the way of the Lord. John 1:19. Notice,

IV. *The Characteristics of His Work and Ministry.*
Look at him,

A. *As a Preacher.*
He stands out eminently in this office. His subjects were,

1. Repentance. His ministry said, Awake to the great concerns of religion, turn from the world to God, hear Jehovah's voice, change your minds and ways—for so the word repentance signifies.
2. Faith in the coming kingdom. "For the kingdom of heaven," etc. The reign of God by the advent of the Lord's anointed is at hand. Prepare for it. Prepare to welcome it. To be blessed by it.
3. He chiefly carried on his ministry in the wilderness of Judea. Here, he published the will of God to the people.
4. His ministry was most faithful. He dealt faithfully with the souls of his hearers: Matthew 3:7,8.
5. His ministry was earnest and devoted. He is described as one "crying." Acting as a herald—lifting up his voice. Crying out and causing the people to know their sins, and Jerusalem her iniquities.

B. *As a Baptizer.*
He not only preached, but he received, and formed into a distinct class, those who received his doctrine and repented of their sins. Hence the disciples of John were baptized in the Jordan, as a sign of their repentance and faith in the coming Messiah. Multitudes thus professed their faith and their expectation of the coming of the Messiah. Matthew 3:5,6. Observe,

V. *The Circumstances of His Eventful Death.*

A. *His ministry was short.*
He labored ardently, and earnestly, and devotedly; but the whole was probably little, if any more, than three years.

B. *His death was connected with the fidelity of his office.*
He was held in general and profound esteem and reverence by the people. Herod, the Tetrarch of Judea, had heard him, and perhaps more than once. Mark 6:20. It is clear, too, that he had consulted him in reference to his marriage to Herodias, his

brother Philip's wife; and John's faithful testimony is recorded, when the preacher said, "It is not lawful for thee to have her," etc. This was the direct link connected with his death.

C. *He died a martyr's violent death.*

See Matthew 14:6ff. There was the festive scene in Herod's palace—a birthday banquet. The company of the lords, high captains, etc. The dancing of Herodias' daughter. Herod's infatuated delight. His absurd promise and imbecile oath. And then the rankling revenge of the odious Herodias. At length the king's demand for the Baptist's head—and its immediate execution.

Application:

1. *Let the theme lead us to meditate on the occasion of John's death.* Matthew 14:12,13. Here is matter for solemn reflection—for grave consideration.
2. *Learn the connection oftentimes between duties and sacrifices.* John might have evaded, and saved his head. He lost his life, and saved the truth, his conscience, his religion, and his soul. "He that loseth his life," etc.
3. *Learn to imitate John in his noble and godly excellence.*
4. *Christians may rejoice in the pre-eminency of their privileges, even over his.*

JABEZ BURNS

THE PALSIED MAN

I. The Need— "One sick of the palsy"— Mark 2:3
"His utter Helplessness— "Born of four"— v. 3

II. The Blessing— "Thy sins be forgiven thee"— v. 5
1. A *divine* forgiveness— "He said"— v. 5
2. A *certain* forgiveness— "He said"— v. 5

III. The cure
1. Sudden— "Immediately he arose"— v. 12
2. Amazing— "They were all amazed"— v. 12
3. Joyful— "Departed . . . glorifying God"— Luke 5:23

INGLIS

JUDAS ISCARIOT

Matthew 27:35

Let us consider,

I. His Character

And observe, that he was,

A. *A follower of Christ*. One who had owned and professed Christ before the world. It is probable that for some time he was externally, at least, a consistent servant of Christ. He was,

B. *An apostle*. One of the twelve. Filled one of the highest offices in Christ's church (Matt. 10:8). No doubt he had every requisite qualification, both as regards knowledge, authority, and miraculous influence. Yet he was,

C. *A hypocrite*. He was a selfish, hollow-hearted character. Gain only, with him, was godliness. His heart was full of lies and deceit. See John 6:66-70; 12:3.

Notice,

II. His Crime

He betrayed and sold his Lord and Master for thirty pieces of silver. This was the climax of his career of iniquity. It was a crime,

A. *Of the greatest treachery*. Although he deserted Christ, he did not become an open foe. Yet, with these marks of attachment, he basely covenanted for his life. It was a crime,

B. *Of the most aggravated wickedness*.

This will appear if you consider,

1. *Who* it was that he betrayed. It was a Friend—a holy, spotless Person—the world's Philanthropist—man's Redeemer—the joy of heaven—and the delight of God.
2. For *what* did he betray Him? For sordid gain—for thirty pieces of silver, the price of a slave.
3. In *what way* did he betray Him? Deliberately made the bargain; coolly executed it; and that with the sacred symbol of love and fidelity—a kiss.

Notice,

III. His Repentance.

It is said, "He repented himself." And here we may observe,

A. *The time*. "When he saw he was condemned." When he beheld the result of his treachery. He was not so much anxious for Christ's death as to obtain the accursed pieces of money. It was characterized,

B. *By sincere sorrow and bitter regret*. He came to the priests with much deep feeling and emotion; his whole soul was evidently affected.

C. *He testified to Christ's innocency and his own guilt*. "I have sinned, in that I have betrayed innocent blood."

D. *He relinquished his ungodly wages*. "He threw down his money," etc. It had been earned too dearly; it was swallowing up all his spirit's happiness; and he cast it entirely away from him. All these things were well; but his repentance was that of remorse, of despair, and of death. He prayed not—he sought not Christ's mercy—made no appeal to God, and exercised neither faith nor hope in Him.

Hence, notice.

IV. His End

His career terminated under the most appalling circumstances. It

A. *Was self-procured*. Having sold his Savior, he murdered himself! Went out to some elevated place and hanged himself; when, most likely the instrument of suspension breaking, he fell down, and his bowels gushed out. His end,

B. *Was hopeless*. He went to his own place. Not that his sin was unpardonable in itself; but instead of fleeing to the only Refuge and the only Deliverer, his remorse was so truly horrific and insupportable, that despairing of mercy he rushed into the presence of the Judge of all, we fear, with all his guilt unpardoned, and on his head, His end,

C. *Was a warning*. Being dead (and we fear lost) he speaks, and says to all men: Beware of hypocrisy; beware of the deceitfulness and hardening influence of sin; beware of covetousness; beware of despondency. "Let me die the death of the righteous," etc.

JABEZ BURNS

MELCHISEDEK

There is a difference between atonement and priesthood—

1. Atonement is a thing of *death*, and priesthood a thing of *life*.
2. Atonement is once for all, *finished*; priesthood is *continuous*.
3. Atonement was accomplished on *earth*; priesthood is carried on in *heaven*.
4. Atonement is for the *sinner*, and priesthood for the *saint*.

Christ is a priest after the order of Melchisedek. Melchisedek was without father or mother in a priestly sense, *i.e.*, his priesthood was of a different order from Aaron's, which depended on descent and genealogy, and lasted for a definite period. Christ is the Eternal One. His priesthood begins and ends with Himself.

It is interesting to note the three things that Melchisedek did when he met Abraham (Gen. 14:18-20).

I. He Brought Forth Bread and Wine to Him.

Bread is strengthening and wine is symbolical of joy. Our High Priest ministers to us His own word and joy.

II. He Blessed Him.

We are blessed in our High Priest. We read that when Christ was about to ascend to heaven, He led His disciples as far as Bethany, and there, with uplifted hands, He blessed them (Luke 24:50). We never read that those hands were put down.

III. He Received from Abraham a Tenth of what he had taken. Our High Priest waits for our gifts and offerings. There are four we can give—

A. Our *bodies* (Romans 12:1).
B. Our *service* (Phil. 2:17; Heb. 13:16).
C. Our *money* (Phil. 4:18).
D. Our *praise* (Heb. 13:15).

F. E. Marsh

THE PARABLE OF THE DAY LABORERS

Matthew 20:1-16

Some have supposed this parable to refer to the various periods of life, when persons are converted and enter into the service of the Lord Jesus Christ. And hence those engaged at the eleventh hour are supposed to refer to persons finding Christ in old age, or on their death-bed. Obviously this was not the message intended by Jesus. The scope of the parable is to show that God in His gracious sovereignty may grant His rewards to those who are late introduced into His vineyard, and whose period of labor is, therefore, of short duration. God may give the same spiritual or eternal blessings to the Gentiles last called, as He did to the Jews; or to the nations who shall be last converted to the faith, as He did to those converted by the apostles. Observe, however, several very important principles which the parable contains.

I. *The Condition, Spiritually, in Which Sinners Live.*

"Idle," during life. "Idle," with the powers and facilities of labor. "Idle," though accountable to God, and notwithstanding His high claims upon their service. With death, and judgment, and eternity before them, still idle as to the work of godliness.

II. *The Great Design of the Christian Ministry Is to Urge Men to Recognize the Duties of Religious Faith.*

Thus they must show men the folly and wickedness of neglecting their souls: that the toils of sin are infinitely more severe and degrading than the service of the Savior; that Christ's labor is sweet and refreshing, and in bearing His yoke, men find rest to their souls. Men must be urged to the work,

A. *Of solemn consideration.*

A review of their past lives, etc. Their present condition. One great reason of men's unconcern is that they do not consider. Hence the requirement of heaven is, "that they consider their ways." Hence the expostulation. Isaiah 1:2,3. Then there is the work,

B. *Of sincere repentance.*

"Repentance towards God." A repentance involving in it conviction of sin—contrition and sorrow for sin—breaking off from sin, and turning to the Lord with full purpose of heart. An entire change of heart and life in respect of sin. See Isaiah 1:16, etc. Where fruits meet for repentance are brought forth.

C. *Of faith in the Lord Jesus Christ.*

Jesus answered and said unto them, "This is the work of God, that ye believe on Him whom He hath sent" (John 6:29). The disciples went and preached that men should repent and believe the gospel.

III. ***That the Church of God Is a Sphere of Labor and Activity.***

Hence Christ's disciples are to be working disciples. Men are introduced into the gospel, not only to enjoy its fruits, but to work therein. True religion is eminently practical. It is the devotion of the heart and life to God. It is walking in the way of His commandments. It is doing the will of our Father in heaven. There are works of devotion—works of self-denial—works of benevolence and mercy. These works are fully specified in the Word of God. And for the discharge of them, sufficient grace is provided.

IV. ***That God Will Reckon with His Servants, and Reward Them When the Day of Labor Is Past.***

Let it not be forgotten that God has a right to all we are, and to all we can do. We never can place the Lord under any obligations by anything we do for Him. But in mercy and goodness to us, He has promised great and munificent rewards to all His faithful servants. There are rewards in God's service, for in keeping His commands, there is great reward. But the chief rewards of godliness,

A. *Are reserved until after death.*

"Be thou faithful unto death," etc. "He that endureth to the end," etc. So in the parable, "when the even was come" (v. 8). The day of life past,

B. *These rewards will be great.*

Not merely equitable remuneration, for what would that be to unprofitable servants? But according to His rich and overflowing mercy, the infinite bountifulness of His nature. These rewards, according to human calculation,

C. *Will not always be proportionate.*

Those hired at the eleventh hour will receive the penny. The last converts, as well as the early ones, will be crowned with glory, immortality, and eternal life. None will receive less than they expected, but many infinitely more. The rewards,

D. *Will be eternal.*

An eternity of rest after toil and peace after the troubles of life. An eternity of joy after grief, and at God's right hand, pleasures for evermore. A crown of glory that fadeth not away. JABEZ BURNS

THE PARABLE OF THE TWO SONS

Matthew 21:28-32

Many of the scribes and Pharisees exhibited the most deep-rooted and inveterate prejudice against the teaching and mission of Jesus. Often they endeavored to catch Him in His sayings, that they might have some charge against Him. Jesus often, therefore, self-convicted them, and out of their own mouths overwhelmed them with confusion. We have a striking instance of this in the passage connected with this subject. To expose their perverseness, the Savior addressed to them this parable, and by their own confessions He involved them in self-condemnation (vv. 31,32). Observe,

I. *The Reasonable Commands of the Father.*

"A certain man had two sons, and he came to the first, and said, Son, go work today in my vineyard" (v. 28). Observe,

A. *The nature of the command.*

"To work in the vineyard." Man was intended for labor. He was made for it. Even in paradise, our first parents were called to it. Labor is dignified and productive, both of health and enjoyment. Hence the command itself was reasonable and proper. God calls men to the great work of personal religion. To work out their own salvation, etc. To give diligence to make their calling and election sure. To work while it is called day. Soul work is all-important, the chief end of life. Observe,

B. *The sphere of labor appointed.*

The father's vineyard. A place in which the sons were personally interested. Now God's vineyard is His church. Into this we are to enter by personal piety, and here we are to improve our graces, employ our talents, do good to men, and glorify God. Has not God a right to specify both the sphere of duty and the labor He demands? Notice,

C. *The manner in which the command was delivered.*

The father said, "Son, go work today," etc. Here was nothing harsh or tyrannical. He speaks with authority, but it is the authority of a parent. He addresses him as his son, and thus conveys the idea of the relationship subsisting between them. As son, he owed his father reverence and cheerful obedience. God is our heavenly Father. We are, therefore, all His offspring. He is not only the Author of our being, but the source of all our mercies. What reverence, obedience, and grateful love we owe to Him. We are not our own but His, for He has not only created and preserved, but redeemed us. Observe,

D. *The period of labor required.*

"Go to work today." Daytime is working time. There is light for working, and opportunity also. The period allotted for labor. God worked during the six days of the creation of our world. "Life is the time to serve the Lord." Jesus said, "I must work while it is called day," etc. What a transient period is the day of life. How soon it passes away. Such were the reasonable requirements of the father, and the claims of God on His creatures. Notice,

II. *The Strange and Diversified Answers of the Sons.*

A. The first said, "I will not." What disobedience, insolence, and rebellion. A direct and impertinent refusal. What baseness, foolhardiness, and ingratitude it involved. Surely of this abandoned son there could be no hope.

B. The second said, "I go, sir." Here was respect, submission, and promised obedience. How forcibly and beautifully it contrasts with the rebellious rudeness of the other. God demands the reverence and fear of His creatures. Divine things and claims must be treated with seriousness and respect. But observe,

III. *The Contrast in Their Conduct.*

A. *The rebellious son becomes penitent and obedient.*

Such were the publicans and sinners to whom John the Baptist preached. So also the publicans and sinners to whom Jesus preached. They notoriously despised sacred things. Abandoned and profligate, yet they repented and obeyed the Baptist, they repented and received salvation from Christ Jesus. How often it has been so. Skeptics—profane scoffers—the openly profane have heard and believed the gospel, to the salvation of their souls. The chief of sinners have been brought to Christ. Zacchaeus, the tax-gatherer. The woman who was a sinner. The dying thief. The Corinthian convert. John Bunyan, the swearing tinker, and myriads of others.

B. *The courteous son was disobedient and deceiving.*

All he did was to be civil and promise fairly. For of him it is said, "He went not." Such were the scribes and Pharisees. They made high pretensions; they professed much, talked much. But, alas! this was all; they said, and did not. It was merely Lord, Lord, in the mouth, but they did not the things which were commanded. They repented not of sin. They believed not in Christ. They were not sincere workers of godliness before the Lord. How fearfully this will apply,

1. To many children of religious parents. They are moral, respectful in their religious conversation, they promise fair, but "go not."

2. To many who regularly frequent the house of God. They attend, and listen, and seem interested; but they are not repentant or holy.

3. It is a faithful picture of many professors. Their religion is in name only—in outward appearance. They are not spiritual, or useful, trees with leaves but no fruit. Ciphers, cumberers of the ground. How fearful this state! How awful their doom!

Learn:

1. The efficacy of the grace of God to save the vilest of sinners.
2. The importance of experiential and practical faith.

JABEZ BURNS

THE PRODIGAL

1.	*Wilful*	"Give me. . . . to me."	Luke 15:12
2.	*Wandering*	"Took. . . . far country."	v. 13
3.	*Wasteful*	"Wasted . . . riotous living."	v. 13
4.	*Wanting*	"He began to be in want."	v. 14
5.	*Wretched*	"He would. . . . did eat."	v. 16
6.	*Welcomed*	"When he . . . kissed him."	v. 20

INCLIS

THE PARABLE OF THE DEBTORS

Matthew 18:23-35

The religion of the New Testament is evidently one of goodness and mercy. Its very essence is love—love to God and love to man. How this was exhibited in the life and doctrines of Jesus Christ! He was the embodiment of goodness—incarnate mercy. He insisted on His disciples cultivating a merciful and forgiving spirit. The kingdom of heaven, or the great principles of the gospel, are beautifully set forth in the figurative sketch before us. Observe,

I. *The King, and the Conduct He Adopted.*

This monarch is represented as having great dignity and wealth. Note also: he took exact observation of the state of his affairs, and the accounts of his servants. He was not indolent or neglectful of the concerns of his kingdom. God is doubtless prefigured in the king before us. He is of boundless authority, riches, and glory. All creatures are under His control, subject to His dominion. He has always an exact knowledge of the state and concerns of all His creatures. His rule is one of exactness, order, and wisdom. Observe,

II. *The Indebted Servant.*

"One was brought unto him who owed him ten thousand talents." This person represented as a servant, doubtless signifies more properly a petty prince, or one employed to collect the revenue in some district of the kingdom. His debts were fearful, "ten thousand talents." If even of silver, a sum upwards of three million pounds sterling, a huge sum in dollars. It is not said how he came to be so deeply involved in debt. He was also entirely insolvent. "He had not to pay his lord." No reference is made even to working out a payment schedule with him. How exactly does this portray the true state of the sinner. He is a debtor to God. His debt is enormous, and he cannot pay the smallest amount. "Poor, and wretched, and blind, and naked." Without God and without hope in the world. Observe,

III. *The Course the King Adopted.*

A. *He reasonably demanded payment*. This was his equitable claim. God requires the yielding of loyal obedience to Him. The perfect love of the heart, and the willing service of the life.

B. *He justly insisted on his punishment*. "Commanded him to be sold," etc. This was the regal right, the understood terms—the covenant between them. God has a just right to punish. He may justly inflict His displeasure. But,

C. *Moved by compassion he freely forgave him.* "The servant, therefore, fell down and worshiped him," etc. (v. 26). The debt was not denied, but acknowledged. His claims were not disputed. But his patience and clemency were prayed for; and moved by noble generosity the king freely and entirely forgave the debt. What an extraordinary instance of compassion. How beautifully does it show the clemency of God to penitent, believing sinners, when they cast themselves on the mercy of God in Christ. Then God, moved by the graciousness of His nature, freely forgives their sins, blotting them out as a cloud. "There is forgiveness with thee," etc. "He who confesseth and forsaketh shall obtain mercy." And no matter how great the debt, He says, "Come now and let us reason together." Notice,

IV. *The Unmerciful Spirit the Forgiven Debtor Displayed.*

"But the same servant went out and found one of his fellow-servants, who owed him a hundred pence, and he laid hands on him," etc. Observe,

A. The debt owed by the fellow-servant was small, "a hundred pence," a tiny amount.

B. He, too, had nothing to pay with, and lacked the ability to meet the demand.

C. He was willing, if time were given, to meet the claim.

D. He humbly and earnestly entreated his compassion.

E. But the pardoned debtor was inexorable. He acted violently, "seized him by the throat," etc.

F. He exercised no forbearance, but at once thrust him into prison (v. 30). What vile forgetfulness of the mercy that had been shown to him! What lack of feeling and sympathy for an unfortunate fellow-creature! Observe, what a picture of man's unmercifulness to man.

V. *The Course Which the King Then Adopted.*

"So when his fellow-servants saw what was done they were very sorry, and came and told unto their lord all that was done. Then his lord, after that he had called him, said unto him, O thou wicked servant," etc. (vv. 31,32). His wickedness was asserted, and the course of conduct he ought to have pursued, pointed out (v. 33). The anger of the king was excited, and in his displeasure he reversed his own merciful decision (v. 34). The conduct of the king as described by Jesus is the precise mode in which God will deal with the unmerciful. "So likewise shall my heavenly Father do also unto you, if ye from your hearts forgive not every man his brother their trespasses" (v. 35). BURNS

THE LOST SHEEP

Luke 15:3-7

The scribes and Pharisees were exceedingly indignant with Christ, because He ate and drank with publicans and sinners. As the professed Messiah, they expected He would treat the profane and irreligious with the contempt and scorn which they displayed toward them. Instead of this, Christ mingled among them, addressed them graciously, and received with open arms all who came in penitence and faith to Him. To justify this course was the design of the parable which He now delivered to them. Observe,

I. ***The Endangered Wanderer.***

The parable supposes a sheep of the fold to have wandered and been lost, a striking and fit description of man's natural condition. This is most forcibly expressed by the evangelical prophet who says, "all we like sheep have gone astray: we have turned every one to his own way" (Isa. 53:6). This is a great doctrinal truth—the fall of man, and the ruin and depravity of the whole species. Prophets, the Lord Jesus, and apostles, all teach and insist on this truth. Man has wandered,

A. *From the authority of God.* Thrown off divine control—said to the Most High, "Depart from us," etc. He is described as despising and ignoring Jehovah. Acting as a traitor and rebel against the sovereign authority of God, he would not have the Lord even in his thoughts. He has wandered,

B. *From the family of God.* He was once in league with holy angels. Most probably they were his companions, we know they were his friends. How holy, and happy, the family of man in innocency. But by apostasy man lost his birthright, became an outcast, etc. His being driven out of Eden was the visible sign of his having wandered from the family of God. Observe,

D. *He has wandered in the way of peril and death.* The tendency of sin is toward death. It is the way of death. Sin, when it is finished, brings forth death. The threatened sentence was, "dying thou shalt die." The wandering sinner is seeking death in the error of his ways. The end of his course is inevitably death. Observe,

E. *The sinner would wander endlessly but for the intervention of divine grace.* There are no desires after God, no holiness in the heart of man by nature. His tendencies are all downward and toward perdition. Satan, who exercises dominion over him, would beguile him, and seduce him away from God and safety. The habit of sinning would greatly increase his love of evil, and his dislike for holy things. Observe then,

II. *The Kindly Shepherd.*

He pities. He seeks. He restores the wanderer. How applicable this to the Savior:

A. *He was compassionate toward man in his fallen and ruined condition*. Hence the scheme of redemption is ever attributed to the pure compassion of God.

"He saw us ruined by the fall,
And loved us notwithstanding all."

"When we were without strength," etc. See Titus 3:3, 7. Compassion moved His heart and induced Him to undertake our recovery and salvation.

B. *He actually came to seek the wanderer*. Jesus left heaven, and laid aside His glory, and became a man—the subject of poverty, and reproach, and suffering, that He might find the wanderer. "This is a faithful saying, and worthy of all acceptation," etc. "The Son of man came to seek and to save that which is lost." For this He lived, and suffered, and died.

C. *He finds and restores the wanderer*. He did so in the days of His flesh. He does so now by the ministry of the gospel. Are not many of you among the number who can sing, "He restoreth my soul"? Among the wanderers found by Christ are sinners of all descriptions, and of all grades of guilt. Some He found in the polluted haunts of profligacy. Others in the mazes of worldliness. Others in the deceitful paths of pleasure. But they were all in the way which leads to death. All would have perished had they not been sought out and found by Him. Observe,

III. *The Joyous Results.*

"And when he hath found it, he layeth it on his shoulders, rejoicing," etc.

A. *The shepherd rejoices in the attainment of his gracious purpose*. He highly values the straying sheep. His best feelings are now gratified. Jesus is represented as seeing the travail of his soul and being satisfied. This was the end of his sorrows and griefs—the joy set before him. In the rescue and elevation of His fallen creatures, His benevolent spirit overflows with rapturous delight.

B. *Angels also rejoice* (v. 7). They are deeply interested in the destiny of man. They have often been messengers of mercy to our world. They hailed the advent of the Savior with great joy. They exult in the sinner's conversion, and they bear the souls of the rescued to the habitations of the blessed. Their love to God, their love of holiness, and their love to man, induce them to rejoice in the sinner's salvation.

C. *The restored wanderer also rejoices*. He sings, "I will praise thee," etc. He invites others to hear what God has done for his soul. He goes on his spiritual way rejoicing. He rejoices with joy unspeakable and full of glory.

D. *All spiritual persons acquainted with the sinner's restoration rejoice*. The minister. The parent. The friend. The church. None but the self-righteous and pharisaic envy and complain. And in proportion to the danger and hopelessness of the sinner's state, is the exultation in his being found by Christ.

We ask in conclusion:

1. *Are you still wandering*? If so, stop! Reflect, and hear the voice of the seeking Savior.
2. *Are you found and restored*? Give God the praise, and glorify Him with your bodies and souls, which are His.

JABEZ BURNS

THREE THINGS ABOUT THE RICH FARMER

I. The ***prosperity*** which favored him.
"No room where to bestow my fruits."— Luke 12:17

II. The ***ungodliness*** which characterized him.
God was not consulted. It was "I," and "My."— vv. 17, 18

III. The ***foolishness*** which he displayed.
This was shown out in three ways:

1. By his promising himself long life.
2. By his preferring the world to Christ.
3. By his preferring time to eternity.

} v. 19, 20

INGLIS

THE PRODIGAL SON

"And He said, A certain man had two sons: and the younger of them said to his father, Father, give me the portion of goods that falleth to me. And he divided unto them his living," etc. (Luke 15:11, 16).

Of all the Savior's parables, this is one of the most interesting and affecting. Surely sin was never painted in more striking colors, or human wretchedness in more piteous strains. And where can we find such an instance of the paternal love and compassion, as is presented to us in the conduct of the father? Let us look at the prodigal,

I. *In His Original Circumstances of Honor and Happiness.*

He was in his father's house the object of paternal affection, bearing the honored name, and moving in the honored rank of his family. This was man's original state—upright, innocent, and happy. God his Father, Eden his home. The earth his domain. Angels his companions. Bliss his portion. All that divine wisdom and love could provide, he possessed. All that he could really enjoy was provided. An ample portion was his inheritance. See him,

II. *In the Arrogance of His Presumptuous Claim.*

What did he really want? Where could he be more dignified or happy? But he seeks to have his portion to himself. He desires to do with it as he pleases. He deems himself sufficient for the management of his own concerns. What was the original sin but throwing off God's restraints, though reasonable and kind, and really for man's good? He desired to act as he pleased, and to have his powers and possessions at his own disposal. Alas! this claim was foolish, ungrateful, and, as the sequel shows, fatal to his hopes and happiness. Observe him,

III. *In His Dissipated Wanderings.*

His portion awarded him, he escapes the parental jurisdiction, and goes into a far country. Sin is the soul's moral departure from God, throwing off His authority. Every step in the course of transgression is going farther and farther from the Lord.

A. This wandering is very gradual and insidious. The moral aberrations are at first small, and only just perceptible. Our first parents gazed on the forbidden tree. Then admired it. Then desired. Then, with the passions on the side of evil, they reasoned and listened to the temptations of the seducer. Then the hand was stretched out. And last of all the fruit was eaten. This is the gradual and insidious course of the sinner. The prodigal would retire at first a day's journey from his home.

B. This wandering is increasingly rapid. The habit and love of evil formed, the course is downward and rapid. Respectability and decency are discarded. Conscience becomes seared—self-respect abandoned. The good opinions of others despised. Now enormous sins are easily perpetrated. No fear of God before the eyes. He can blaspheme—mock at sin. Be the hearty associate of the vilest of the vile. He is sold, body, soul, and spirit, to do wickedly.

C. This wandering is dangerous. It is the way of shame, misery, and death. It leads to an early grave. Observe the prodigal,

IV. ***In His Wretchedness and Misery.***

"He had spent all" (v. 14). Sin is fearfully expensive. Let the experience of the profligate certify to the truth of this. Pride, ambition, profligacy, are all ruinous. "He spent all." A rich portion was gone—rapidly and foolishly. Now comes the moral death—famine. The means are exhausted. He begins now to be "in want." Profligacy is followed by want, extravagance by misery. This is the history of millions. Behold him,

V. ***In His Unalleviated Distress.***

The proud prodigal becomes a swineherd, the most degrading and miserable of all occupations. What filthy employment Satan gives his slaves to do! How iniquity degrades and debases! It is a constantly falling state—men sink lower and lower, until, covered with infamy, their souls commingle with the vile and the lost in the abyss of woe beneath. Even swine's food is not given him (v. 16). By husks is meant the fruit of the carob-tree, which was used in feeding swine, and on which the most poor and wretched were compelled to live.

Where are his evil friends? Why not go to the haunts of his former pleasures and rioting? Sin is a cruel, hardening thing. Sinners victimize one another. They rob and destroy each other. "The tender mercies of the wicked are cruel." There is no aliment of life and comfort in the region of sin. Ah! the contrast between the prodigal's state now and when at home in the midst of plenty and comfort. Look at his wan and pallid countenance. Look at his ragged, filthy dress. See him at his cursed employment. For cursed, said one of the Rabbins, "is he that feedeth swine." See him seeking the meanest fare in vain, and what is the conclusion to which we must come? "The way of transgressors is hard." "It is a hard and bitter thing to sin against the Lord."

JABEZ BURNS

THE PRODIGAL SON (II)

"And when he came to himself, he said, How many hired servants of my father have bread enough and to spare, and I perish with hunger! I will arise and go to my father, and will say unto him, Father, I have sinned against heaven and before thee . . . " (Luke 15:17, 20).

We have seen in our previous discourse the prodigal in his original state of happiness, in his wanderings, and in his utter wretchedness. We have now to contemplate him under the favorable circumstances, which took place at the very crisis of his misery and distress. Far from home. In a degraded service. In utter destitution. Without friends or sympathy in his misfortunes, and exclaiming, "I perish with hunger." But the darkest part of his career is now passed; his misery drives him to reflection, for observe,

I. *Reason Resumes Her Dominion.*

"And when he came to himself." His course had been one of madness, insanity, delirium. Was it not so to throw off the paternal yoke of wisdom and love? Was it not so to trust to his own inexperience? Was it not so to go out into a far and unknown region—without object, or counselor, or guide? Was it not so to waste a life's substance in a few years? Was it not so to become the companion of harlots and thieves? Surely all this was evidence of the direst infatuation, the most obvious madness. All sin is madness, the opposite of sound reason, of true wisdom.

A. To reject and despise God.
B. To prostitute the powers of the soul to evil.
C. To neglect the great end of life.
D. To be indifferent to our own welfare.
E. To disregard the certain solemnities of death, judgment, and eternity. But the prodigal came to himself.
   1. For behold, he stops in his career of vice to consider. He now soliloquizes with himself.
   2. He now thinks of the home he had despised. "How many hired servants," etc.
   3. He now perceives distinctly, and confesses frankly his own condition. "I perish with hunger." In these we see the first indications of the return of a good understanding and a sound judgment. Happy sign,

when the sinner pauses and begins to consider. Men perish because they do not, they will not consider. Consideration is the herald of repentance and the bringer of reformation.

Observe,

II. ***The Resolution Which He Adopts.***

He determines,

A. *On an immediate return to his forsaken home.* "I will arise," etc. (v. 18). It is evident from the very language he employs, that this resolution is the result of deep conviction. He decides to travel no longer in the way of sin and death. He has already repented, changed his mind, and changed his position; his face is now set toward home. His eyes are in the right direction; his mind is made up. He resolves to return, and to do so at once.

How necessary is such a resolution! For the want of it many have wavered and halted until the door of hope has closed. Let such a resolution be formed in connection with earnest prayer, for the Divine help, in firm confidence that God will give grace for its performance.

B. *He resolves freely to confess his sins.* "And will say, Father, I have sinned," etc. (v. 18). His confession is frank and open. By my ingratitude, he says, I have been foolish, base, and wicked. I now see it, know it, feel it, deplore it, and confess it. I hate myself for it. I am full of self-loathing and self-condemnation. How striking and full this confession! How the very purpose of it must have relieved his wretched, guilty spirit!

C. *He resolves to be content with any place in his father's dwelling.* "And am no more worthy to be called thy son," etc. (v. 19). He had forfeited the family name; he had no claim to be reinstated in his original place, having squandered the portion allotted to him. He is willing to become a servant. Better far to be a servant of his father than the servile herdsman of swine. Such are the feelings of the sin-convicted soul. The soul is prostrated in the dust. The least of God's mercies is earnestly desired. He is willing to be anything or to do anything for the Lord.

III. ***The Course Which He Promptly Carries Out.***

"And he arose," etc. (v. 20).

A. *Immediately, without delay.* At once. He did not

defer it to another season. His misery, his danger, urged him to action. His feelings were intense, so that at once "He arose," etc. How many have perished for want of immediate action! Their views have been correct, convictions have been experienced, resolutions formed; but then, delay has followed, and these delays have been increased, until the harvest has ended, and until the day has expired, until it has been too late. "Today, therefore, if ye will hear His voice," etc. "Behold, now is the accepted time," etc.

B. *He persevered in his homeward course.* He resolutely set out, and retraced his steps. He allowed nothing to divert him. Hindrances to the repentant sinner will be presented. But the course of penitential return must be pursued; the language of the soul must be, "Hinder me not." The ears must be closed, as in the case of Bunyan's Pilgrim, and the cry must be, "Eternal life! eternal life!!"

Happy change! He now enters on the region of hope. We ask, in conclusion:

1. How many present know the prodigal's repentance, in their own experience!
2. Who will now consider his ways, and turn to the Lord with full purpose of heart?
3. There must be repentance, or inevitable death.

JABEZ BURNS

THE WOMAN WITH AN INFIRMITY

I. Her condition Described
1. Its *origin*— "Sin"— Luke 13:16
2. The *agent*— "Satan"— v. 16
3. Its *nature*— "Bondage"— v. 16
4. *Its duration*— "Eighteen years"— v. 16

II. The Change She Experienced
1. It was a *speedy* change— vv. 13, 14
2. It was a *public* change— vv. 13, 14

INGLIS

THE PRODIGAL SON (III)

"And he arose and came to his father. But when he was yet a great way off, his father saw him, and had compassion, and ran, and fell on his neck, and kissed him: and the son said unto him, Father, I have sinned against heaven, and in thy sight, and am no more worthy to be called thy son," etc. (Luke 15:20, 32).

We have now to contemplate the most beautiful part of this moral picture. The prodigal is nearing, and we witness the happy results of true repentance, and spiritual reformation of life. His mind is full of anxiety—his heart throbbing with the conflicting emotions of shame, penitence, and hope. The Savior introduces the father to us, as if he had been looking toward the country to which the prodigal had wandered. No doubt his heart had often yearned over his wicked and disobedient child. Observe then,

I. ***The Happy Meeting.***

In this meeting there is much of minute detail, that must not be overlooked.

A. *The father first saw the prodigal.* He beheld him when yet at a considerable distance. Saw him in his rags and misery; yet saw him returning—knew him as his rebellious child, but now with his rebellious heart subdued.

God, our gracious Father, sees the first dawn of spiritual light in the sinner's mind. He witnesses his feet returning toward the way of obedience and life.

B. *The father ran to meet the prodigal.* Does not withdraw himself, nor even to wait for the penitent obeisance of his child. Full of love, he hastens to meet him, and thus to inspire him with hope and joy. Just so God seeks the wandering sinner—beseeches him to come to Him, and live. Says, "Come now and let us reason," etc. (Isa. 1:18, etc.).

C. *The father exhibits the reconciled state of his heart toward him.* "And had compassion, and ran, and fell on his neck," etc. The father moved first in this reconciliation. It was his very nature. He delighted to exhibit it. How free—how full—how spontaneously it flowed. He embraces him. He gives him the token of his pardon and favor, for he kisses him. And now, observe,

D. *The prodigal's confession.* His father's mercy and tender preventing love did not satisfy the prodigal, or render his repentance and confession the less, but rather the more necessary. His remorse would be doubled, his sorrow the more intense at having offended, despised, and forsaken such a father. So he said, "Father, I have sinned," etc. The goodness of God generally leads to repentance. It is the cross of Christ that subdues the heart. The graciousness of the gospel that gives it its saving power. Observe,

II. *The Hearty Reception.*

We have seen him already in the father's arms and bosom. Observe, now, the train of blessings which he receives.

A. *His rags are exchanged for the family costume.* "The best robe is put upon him." God has appointed to those that mourn in Zion, "Beauty for ashes, the oil of joy for mourning, the garment of praise for the spirit of heaviness" (Isa. 61:3). See Psalm 30:11.

B. *The ring of acceptance is placed on his finger.* This is the sign, and token, and pledge of pardon, and reconciliation. It would remind him both of his wanderings and adoption.

C. *God gives his spirit to testify to the penitent sinner's acceptance. Shoes* are *placed* on his feet. Servants and slaves generally worked barefoot. This showed, therefore, that he was received as a son, and not as a hired servant. Shoes are the emblem of filial obedience and love. Notice,

III. *The Distinguished Banquet.*

"And bring hither the fatted calf," etc. (v. 23). Here was a festival of joy and gladness. The gospel dispensation is often likened to a feast. It was predicted as such. See Isaiah 25:6,7. The Savior compared it also to a feast (Matt. 20:1, 4). Observe,

A. *The provision was abundant.* The richest and best the family could provide.

B. *The guests were numerous.* The tidings of the returned prodigal were soon spread abroad, and neighbors and friends were invited to share in the joy of the occasion.

C. *The rejoicing was great.* A lost son found, a dead son alive! If the finding of a lost piece of money, or recovering a wandering sheep, should give joy—how much more the restoration of an immortal mind. Salvation of a deathless being, the recovery of a prodigal child. What joy should the restoration of a fallen sinner produce on earth, when the very angels of God are enraptured and exult on the occasion. The parable concludes,

IV. *With the Cold-hearted Envy of the Elder Brother.*

Here, doubtless, was portrayed the spirit of the Jews in general, in their dislike of the Gentiles, but more especially the envy of the Pharisees, that Christ should receive publicans and sinners. The spirit of the elder brother,

A. *Was base and inhuman.* For the occasion of the joy, was his brother—his younger brother. He refuses him, however, that appellation, and calls him, "Thy son."

B. *It was self-righteous.* He describes himself as faultless. "Neither transgressed I at any time" (v. 29). Who can truly say that? Let him who is without sin cast the first stone. How striking the contrast of the spirit of the father, and of the elder brother! How forcibly, yet sweetly, he replies to his unkind and envious remarks! How he dwells on the interesting character of the occasion! How he defends the joy and gladness which was exhibited!

Learn:

1. *How generous and pure is the benevolence of the gospel.* It is of God, and from him, and resembles his tender and infinite love.
2. *How hateful is an envious self-righteous spirit.* It is the spirit of the evil one, and therefore, from beneath.
3. *Happy they who have repented of sin, and who have been received into the Savior's family of love.*

JABEZ BURNS

A FIVEFOLD VIEW OF PAUL

1. His Humility
   "Lease of all saints."— Eph. 3:8
2. His Qualification
   "Is this grace given."— Eph. 3:8
3. His Commission
   "That I should preach."— Eph. 3:8
4. His Sphere
   "Among the Gentiles."— Eph. 3:8
5. His Theme
   "The unsearchable riches of Christ."— Eph. 3:8

INGLIS

PARABLE OF THE UNPROFITABLE SERVANT

(Luke 17:7, 10)

How important it is that we should have correct views of the divine claims upon us, and the spirit in which those claims should be met. We can err as to our duty through ignorance, or as to the manner of performing it, through the pride which is within us. It is clear that God does not require meritorious services from us in order to our acceptance with Him, yet He does require the obedient homage of all who are accepted of Him. The sacrifice of Christ alone is the ground of our acceptance—the evidence of it, the fruits of practical godliness. The parable illustrates the nature of the service God requires. The support He affords in it. And the divine independency with respect to it. Observe,

I. *The Nature of the Service God Requires.*

It is indicated by the labors of the servants who are described as "ploughing or feeding cattle." That is, doing His work. Attending to His concerns. Doing His bidding. And this He,

A. *Has revealed in His Word.* A knowledge of His statutes will make us acquainted with His will and our duty. Personal, social, and public duties, are all revealed here. The duties we owe immediately to Him, to His people, and to the world. The whole province of obedience is mapped out in His Holy Word.

B. *For this He has given us the capacity and powers which are essential.* In His laws He has consulted our abilities and powers. He demands nothing that cannot be fully yielded. He seeks only according to the ability He bestows, and expects a return just in proportion to the talents committed to our trust. The obedience He claims must possess the following characteristics.

1. It must be the obedience of *love*. Not of terror or constraint. Not servile—but affectionate. "This is the love of God, that we keep His commandments," etc.

2. It must be *spiritual*. There must be the act, and also the spirit in the action performed. No service will please Him which is not spiritual.

3. It must have *respect* to all His commandments. It must be *entire*—obeying all His will.

4. It must be *constant*. The habit of the life. The daily course. In all things seeking to please Him.

5. It must be *persevering* devotion unto death. Working to the end of the day of life. Observe,

II. ***The Support He Gives in It.***

This is implied in His sitting down to "eat and drink" (v. 7,8). Notice,

A. *God gives ability for the service.* The daily strength is imparted by Him. All our power and sufficiency is of God. We can do all things through Christ, who strengthens us.

B. *He provides daily food for the soul.* The bread of life, and the waters of salvation. Grace according to the day. Food to eat, of which the world knows nothing. The rich and sufficient blessings of the gospel.

C. *He gives satisfaction and peace in the service.* "They have great peace who keep Thy law," etc. The peace of faithful servants flows as a river. A satisfaction and joy, sweet and unspeakable.

All proper labor is profitable, but the service of God especially and pre-eminently. "Godliness is profitable," etc. But there is also,

D. *The joy arising from the hope of reward.* Unto the servants of the Lord are given exceeding great and precious promises. Promises of future and eternal glory. His faith often anticipates the glory that shall be revealed, and the crown that does not fade away. "I know whom I have believed," etc. Notice,

III. ***The Divine Independency with Respect to This Service.***

Does the master thank "that servant because He did the things that were commanded," etc. (v. 9)? Now the force of this will be seen when it is remembered,

A. *That no man can go beyond the divine claims in his obedience.* God claims the entire obedience of body, soul, and spirit. So that works beyond capability are literally impossible.

B. *God's goodness to man is ever beyond the services He receives from him.* So that man must by necessity ever be a debtor to God.

C. *That man's best services are, because of his infirmities, frail and imperfect.* Thus, he must ever be the subject of the divine forbearance and long-suffering. "For He knoweth our frame, and remembereth that we are dust." It is only through the virtue of the Savior's mediation, that either the person or obedience of man can be accepted of the Lord. How fitting then that they should say, "We are unprofitable servants: we have done that which was our duty to do" (v. 10).

JABEZ BURNS

PAUL'S EXPERIENCE

Acts 26:5-26

I. Conversion of Paul.

The Apostle tells Agrippa what he *was* when in his natural state; namely, a self-righteous Pharisee (v. 5), and opponent to Jesus (v. 9), a persecutor of the saints (v. 10), a misguided man in obeying the priests (v. 10), an inflicter of punishment upon God's people (v. 11), an instrument in the hands of Satan in causing some of the disciples of Christ to blaspheme (v. 11), and a fanatic, in that he was "exceedingly mad" in his unholy service (v. 11); but a vision of Christ in His holiness caused him to see his sinfulness. It was Paul's *obedience* to the heavenly vision that was the pivot upon which the persecutor became the pleader with God and men (v. 19).

II. Commission of Paul.

Being *saved* through Christ he was next *sent* by Christ to preach the Gospel. We are saved to serve, we do not serve to be saved. Paul was sent to accomplish a fivefold purpose in the power of the Holy Spirit (v. 18).

Revelation. "Open their eyes."
Repentance. "Turn from darkness to light."
Release. "From the power of Satan unto God."
Remission. "Receive forgiveness of sins."
Riches. "Inheritance."

All these blessings are bestowed upon those who have faith in Christ.

III. Consecration of Paul.

"I was not disobedient," etc. (v. 19). Obedience is the law of the Kingdom of Grace.

IV. Continuance of Paul (v. 22).

The Apostle tells us the secret of his continuance: it was because he obtained (not attained) help from God. *Obtainment* is the secret of *attainment*. Mark that the Apostle obtained help for a specific object, viz., that he might witness to and of the things in the Scriptures.

V. Creed of Paul (v. 23).

He believed in the sufferings of Christ for the sins of man, and in the resurrection of Christ for the justification of the believer (Rom. 4:25).

VI. Calmness of Paul (v. 25).

Festus thinks that Paul is mad as he listens to the earnest and burning words which fall from his lips, and tells him so; but, as the Apostle says, he is perfectly cool and calm, and speaks forth "the words of truth and soberness."

VII. Courage of Paul (v. 26).

The Apostle does not hesitate to tell King Agrippa that he knew what he was speaking about, and then begins to put pointed questions to him. Courage is one of the fruits of the filling of the Holy Spirit (Acts 4:31).

F. E. MARSH

THE PHILIPPIAN JAILER

I. An Important Questioned Asked

"What must I do to be saved?"— Acts 16:30

The jailer was evidently:

1. A *lost* man— "His anxiety was for salvation."— v. 30
2. An *awakened* man— "Awaking out of his sleep."— v. 30
3. An *ignorant* man— "What must I do?"— v. 30
4. An *convicted* man— "Came trembling."— v. 29

II. A Truthful Answer Given

"Believe . . . saved."— Acts 16:31

The person to believe in.— "The Lord Jesus Christ."

III. The Blessed Results Which Followed

1. He was *saved*— "Believe in God."— v. 34
2. He was *obedient*— "Was baptized."— v. 33
3. He *rejoiced*— "And rejoiced."— v. 34

INGLIS

PAUL'S HAPPY EXPERIENCE

2 Timothy 1:12

Notice,

I. **The Apostle's Happy Retrospect**

"I know whom I have believed," etc.

A. He had believed in Christ.

The circumstances connected with his conversion are fully detailed; how he was arrested on his way to Damascus—his blindness, visit of Ananias, baptism, etc; his confession of his own life: "I am crucified with Christ, nevertheless I live, yet not I, but Christ liveth in me; and the life that I live in the flesh, I live by the faith of the Son of God, who loved me, and gave Himself for me" Galatians 2:20.

B. He had committed his soul to Christ, that He might save it, keep it, sanctify it. He had consecrated all his powers to promote His honor and glory in the world. He had devoted his all to Christ, and that forever. "Yea, doubtless, and I count all things but loss . . ." "God forbid that I should glory . . ."

C. He was experimentally satisfied with the object of his faith and trust. "I know whom I have believed . . ."

II. **His Joyous Prospect**

"And I am persuaded that He is able to keep what I have committed Him," etc.

A. His prospect related to his preservation.

That he should be kept; that his solemn deposit would be perfectly secure. And, if our souls are in Christ's hands who shall harm them? Who can pluck them out? They shall be kept from all evil, and raised to eternal life.

B. His prospect rested on Christ's ability. "That He is able to keep."

Yes, all power is His, both in heaven and on earth. "Able to save to the uttermost." His arm never wearies, for it is girt with omnipotence.

C. His prospect extended to the judgment-day.

"Against that day." Day of solemn examination; day of destiny and doom; day of signal honor and reward to the saints.

Application:

1. True religion is founded on knowledge. The Christian

knows himself, and he knows Jesus Christ. The knowledge of his own misery had led him to value and accept the fullness of Christ.

2. True religion must be matter of personal experience. We must have the light of it in our minds, and the feeling sense of it in our hearts. It must be a matter of happy consciousness.
3. True religion ensures safety. Yes, the saints shall be kept by the power of God to eternal salvation.
4. True religion is full of hope. It gives a persuasion of public acceptance and distinction at the last day.

JABEZ BURNS

PAUL THE "PATTERN"

Paul's confession (1 Tim. 1:15).

Paul's persuasion (Rom. 8:38).

Paul's determination (1 Cor. 2:2).

Paul's pleasures (2 Cor. 12:10).

Paul's learning (Phil. 4:11).

Paul's glory (Gal. 6:14).

Paul's exhortation (1 Cor. 15:58).

Paul's farewell (2 Tim. 4:7,8, 22).

PAUL OBTAINING MERCY

1 Timothy 1:16

I. The Apparent Difficulties in the Way of Paul Finding Mercy

In the previous verse he calls himself the chief of sinners.

A. He was entirely ignorant of the plan of salvation. He was a Pharisee in heart, profession, and life. No idea that he was a sinner—no idea of divine mercy—no idea of contrition, of self-abasement. He trusted in his own righteousness, in the goodness of his own heart. Now, there is but one plan of salvation. Through the mercy of God, and by faith in the Messiah.

B. He was an unbeliever.

He lived at a most eventful crisis. Just when the Spirit had been poured down from on high. The events concerning Jesus and His crucifixion, together with the doctrines of the apostles, must have been familiar to him. Yet, like thousands of his countrymen, he closed his eyes against the light, his ears against the truth, and his heart against the influence of the gospel.

C. He was a blasphemer.

See verse 18. Openly vilified the name of Jesus.

D. He was a bitter persecutor.

His soul burned with unhallowed zeal against Christ and His cause. It is said, he breathed threatenings against the disciples, Acts 9:1. His soul was inflamed with the fire of hellish hate, etc. See Acts 22:4; also 8:3. He was one who saw the first martyrs in Christ's cause expire. See Acts 7:57-59.

E. He was injurious.

This we have already exemplified in his character as a persecutor; but it is likely that, in addition to all this, he blasted the reputation of the saints, and thus sacrificed their good names, as well as their property, liberty, and life. Or, it may signify, that as a persecutor, he was remarkably successful in distressing and injuring the friends of Christ. Such, then, were the apparent difficulties in the way of Paul's conversion. Observe,

II. The Mercy Which He Obtained

Mercy is the exercise of favor to the guilty and unworthy.

A. He obtained sparing mercy.

B. He obtained pardoning mercy.
C. He obtained renewing mercy.
D. He obtained exalting, distinguishing mercy.

Sin had plunged him deeply into wretchedness and misery. The grace of God exalted him as highly.

E. He obtained sustaining and preserving mercy.

III. The Great Ends Christ Had in View in Imparting Mercy to Paul

A. He exhibited His own long-suffering. How easily He could have disarmed the mad youth. How easily have broken him in pieces as a potter's vessel. But patience prevailed, etc. He was not indifferent—no! He felt every attack as done to Himself, etc.

B. He exhibited the freeness and power of His grace. To whom will He now deny it? On whom can it prove ineffectual when it has saved Paul?

C. As a pattern of the way of salvation to all.

Application:
Learn,

1. The sovereign power and grace of God. All resources and instruments are His. "He maketh His enemies," etc.
2. The encouragement the subject affords to the greatest of sinners. Yes, Jesus died for the chief of sinners. None need despair.
3. The connection of faith with eternal glory.
4. The great business of believers. To magnify divine grace. Let us sing of divine mercy. Talk of it. Recommend it.

JABEZ BURNS

PAUL'S RAPTURE AND HUMILIATION

2 Corinthians 12:1

The text refers to one of the most remarkable events in the life of the great apostle; yet it has to do with the inner life and experience. He relates it to show, in spite of the depreciating attempts of some, that he has the most extraordinary reasons of glorying, were it proper to do so, in the abundance of the revelation with which he had been favored.
Observe—

I. The Character of His Own Piety

"A man in Christ." Knowing Christ; believing in Christ; savingly united to Christ; in Christ. As Noah was in the ark. As the man-slayer was in the city of refuge. As the branch is in the vine. We may hear of Christ, be near to Christ; but Paul was in Christ. "If any man be in Christ," etc.

II. His Reference to Past Experience

"Fourteen years ago." "Thou shalt remember all the way thy God hath led thee," etc. How profitable to do so! A year, how fruitful in events! But fourteen years in the life and labors of the great apostle, how momentous in results! He refers—

III. To the Extraordinary Events in That Experience

His mysterious condition (v. 2). Evidently in a trance. Lost to the things of earth and time. Body chained down. Spirit soaring upwards and free. He was caught up into the "third heaven," "Paradise." To the Hades of the blest. "Spirit world of the happy." Where Jesus is more immediately manifested. He had marvelous revelations (v. 4). "Not lawful," not possible or proper to utter, etc. Not to be told to men, etc.
Look—

IV. At the Design of This

No doubt—

- A. *To honor the apostle*. Midst the shame, etc., to which he was exposed.
- B. *To reward the apostle* for the loss of the things he had sacrificed for Jesus.
- C. *To inspire the joyful hope of the apostle* in his arduous career.

Observe—

V. The Peril of This

Verse 7. In danger of being "exalted above measure." Become proud, or vain, or self-sufficient. No doubt Satan felt thus. How often we see this effect produced by riches, rank, popularity. Sometimes religion is perverted to effect the same, spiritual pride, etc. Now, this was the peril involved, which included his reason, his happiness, his soul.

Notice then—

VI. How the Apostle Was Preserved

Verse 7. "And lest," "a thorn in the flesh," etc. The word denotes a prickly briar, sharp, painful. All sorts of guesses have been made as to what it was. Some have thought it a painful bodily disease. Defective utterance. Constant attacks of the evil one. Slanderous oppression of his enemies. False teachers, etc. God often sends correctives, preservatives. He sees some in danger of worldliness, and sends adversity. Human popularity and applause, and He allows some slanderous reptile to crawl over their reputation. Creature idolatry, and He sends the black postman of death, etc. Hardness and indifference, and He sends severe and alarming illness to soften, etc.

VII. The Results of the Divine Arrangement

Paul refers to—

A. *His devotional ardor* (v. 8). Three agonizing conflicts. "Prayed thrice."
B. *The inward assurance* of sufficient grace (v. 9, etc.).
C. *Joyful submission*. "Most gladly," etc.

VIII. Learn—

A. How the most eminent are in danger.
B. How the best may suffer.
C. How grace is ever sufficient, etc.

JABEZ BURNS

THE RICH FARMER

Luke 12:20

It is obvious, from the connotation of the text, that the man was lost through being a covetous secularist. See verse 15. Let us then consider,

I. **His Circumstances**

These are described in one word. He was rich, prosperous. His ground brought forth plentifully. External prosperity is no sign either of the divine approbation or displeasure. One thing, however, is very certain, that it is a state of imminent danger. We read of three striking cases in the Word of God,

A. *A youth, whom riches kept from being a disciple of Christ* (Mark 10).

B. *A professor, whom riches destroyed.* Demas (2 Tim. 4:10; Col. 4:14; Philem. 24). etc., and then,

C. *The worldling in the text,* whose mind was entirely absorbed, so that religion had no place whatever in this thoughts. It is difficult to be prosperous and rich,

1. Without loving riches. The love of money, etc. Whoso loveth the world, etc.
2. Without thinking ourselves the better and greater for riches. How they puff up the mind. How men glory in their profession.
3. Without trusting in riches and not in God. There is danger when full, of denying Him.

II. **His Character**

God gives it, therefore, it must be correct. "Thou fool." Now, his folly is seen in the following particulars:

A. *In being anxious amidst profusion.* We say to that poor man, be not anxious: but the grace of God only can make him happy in poverty. But when you have riches, why be so? When you are full to overflowing, why be so? Yet he was (v. 17). How different from others, they had room but no fruits, no goods. Blessings not sent to be laid up. No; but to be diffused abroad. He was a fool,

B. *Because he expected his soul to be happy with temporal things* (v. 19). His soul had no appetite for temporal things. It wanted a good suited to its nature. The soul is a spirit, an immortal, immaterial principle, and it must have spiritual food, or starve and die. But he tried to make an earthworm of his soul. He wished to grovel in the dust.

C. *Because he presumptuously calculated on years to come.* The uncertainty of life is most evident. Yet, this is the folly, that all men think all men mortal but themselves. Listen to this reckless boaster, "This will I do." Do not be presumptuous. Is it not better to say, If the Lord will? "Soul, thou hast," etc., "for many years." "Boast not thyself of tomorrow. Thou knowest not," etc. Man is a thing of naught, his breath is in his nostrils, etc. Notice, then,

III. His End

God saw him, and heard him; and then addressed him, "Thou fool, this night," etc.

A. *His end was sudden and unexpected.* "This night." In the midst of riches; in the midst of plans; in the midst of hopes.

B. *For his end he was unprepared.* He had prepared for his fruits, for the body, and for time; but not at all for the soul, and for eternity. These neglected, unprepared for, etc.

C. *His end was dreadfully momentous.* His soul was required. By whom? By God. For what? Examination. Judged for its eternal destiny. The books are opened. The trial. The sentence—all awaits you.

Application:

1. Do not idolize and trust in riches.
2. Be anxious for your soul's welfare.
3. Come to Jesus. He will make you wise to eternal life.
4. Do not presume. Do not calculate upon the future.

JABEZ BURNS